WHERE BEAUTIFUL INKS
Unrequited
POETRY AND PROSE

WRITTEN BY:
BRANDY LANE

FORT WAYNE, INDIANA

© 2023 Unrequited Poetry and Prose

Author: Brandy Lane
Editor: Valerie Lorraine

All rights reserved.
Printed in the United States of America.

No part of this book may be used, stored in a system retrieval system, or transmitted, in any form or any means—by electronic, mechanical, photocopying, recording, or reproduced in any manner whatsoever—without written permission from the author, except in the case of brief quotations embodied in critical articles and reviews.

Published in the United States of America by
Where Beautiful Inks LLC

Fort Wayne, Indiana

ISBN: 978-1-7363268-5-5

Library of Congress Control Number: 2023922653

All pictures throughout this book are available through Canva and Canva Pro.

Dedication

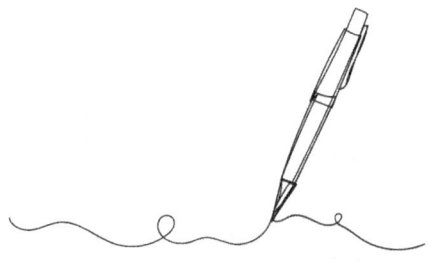

Awakening feelings of being lost—
or more like having lost something
or someone.
The angst of losing myself whilst
trying to forget you.

A Letter to My Muse

It's gloomy today,
the pitter-patter of rain is a welcome company...

My words have not been flowing like they used to. Almost a stutter in my mind. They get stuck within my chest even though I'm writing and not speaking. I'm uncertain where these stones came from, if I put them there, or if I'm not supposed to share.

I want to so badly that it aches.

I feel forgotten by most of the world, but I'm certain I'm not the only one who feels this way. At least if things were never to be as they were, I have beautiful memories.

I often think of the first time we came to your house to play games; you introduced me and said, "This is my friend Brandy—we love each other!"

I will never forget that.

It was the best compliment I'd ever received—a declaration of love to everyone.

I smile whenever I remember any lovely moment I've had with you, and then I weep, because I want to always feel that closeness.

I have said it before, and it still holds true;

> "I'd rather have this ache in my chest, than the nothing I felt before."

Because this ache means that I am capable of love, this ache means that I have felt loved, this ache means that without you in my life... I have a void that cannot be filled by any other means, nor would I want a substitute.

I'm still here, just contemplative and longing for your company. I tell you this not to cause you angst but to bring joy in knowing that you are loved and not alone in spirit.

Alfred Lloyd Tennyson said:

> "It is better to have loved and lost than to have never loved at all."

I'm grateful for the time that I was allowed to slightly obsess over you... to treat you as though you were on a pedestal. I will always know you as one of the greatest romances I've ever known, and I sincerely hope we can remain friends in this weary world. I may have gotten carried away, but I will admit, I didn't just fall for you, I skydived.

Forever and Always,

Brandy

Table of Contents

Funny 2

Too Late 3

Empty 4

Homeless 5

My Heart 6

Say Goodbye 7

All Alone 8

Alive 9

Owned 10

I Refrain 11

Whole 12

To Be Held 13

Soul Mate 14

I Love You 16

War Cry of the Valkyrie 17

All I Ever Needed 18

Love has Flown 20

Loaded Gun 21

Smile, then Cry 22

Tell Me 23

Back Home 24

Walk With Me 25

Moving On 26

Empty House 28

Lonely 30

Bound 32

Sweet and Hot 34

Yin and Yang 35

Don't You Fret 36

Spill 38

I Knew You When 39

My Last "I Love You" 40

Just in Case 41

Dying Embers 42

Overwinter 43

No Longer 44

What's the Point? 46

Yours 48

Obsession 50

Where is the Joy? 51

Intoxicate 52

Flesh and Bones 53

Ache 54

My Love in Ruins 56

Ruined 57

Nothing Compares 58

It's Over 59

Words 60

I Will Never Be Fine 61

Never 62

Vastly Different Things 63

Don't Play for Me 64

Almost Love 66

I Simply Love You 68

Thinking of You 69

Fallen 70

I Already Know 71

Never Again 72

In Pause 73

Love Isn't Enough 74

In Your Arms 75

I Want to be Kissed 76

Unbroken 77

Queen of my Dreams 78

I am Cassandra 79

Alien 80

Minstrel 81

Loving a Ghost 82

Into My Soul 84

First Kiss 85

Dismay 86

Does God Write Poetry? 87

My Love 88

Adorned in You 89

Dream of You 90

Never Just a Muse 91

The Rabbit 92

Contented 93

Chosen Family 94

Pieces of Me 95

Desire 96

Dream 97

Already Yours 98

Just One More 99

She Really Loves You 100
Stranded 101
Wardrobe 102
Guilt 104
The Day I Met You 105
Like an Addict 106
No Longer 107
Bittersweet 108
Think of Me 109
Chaos 110
You are All I See 111
Oxygen 112
Starved 113
Without Fail 114
The Corner 115
Remembering 116
Naked Walls 118
Despondent 119
Smirk 120
Here to Mourn 121
Tokatsubo 122
No Longer in Denial 124
Stupid 125
Just a Breath 126
Compass 127
Your Favorite Book 128
Turn 129
Unloved 130
Gravity 131

Concupiscence ... 132

Confession ... 133

Whispered Love ... 134

Haunt ... 135

My Heart Breaks ... 136

Enough ... 137

Truly Wanted ... 138

Wild Abandonment ... 139

Mind to Mind ... 140

Unbreakable ... 141

I Always Will ... 142

Him ... 143

Fading ... 144

Balconies ... 146

Hibernation ... 148

Vanquish ... 149

Halfway Blooming ... 150

Without ... 152

Promise ... 154

I Close My Eyes ... 156

Temptation ... 158

If My Soul Could Speak ... 159

Forbidden ... 160

Syncopation ... 161

I Miss You ... 162

Without You ... 164

Time With You ... 165

Echo ... 166

Being There 168
Piece of Art 169
Just Like You 170
Wild Things 173
Teardrops 174
The Train 175
Irreplaceable 176
Pieces of Me 177
Dragon Tears 178
Awaiting a Frolic 180
Happy Endings 181

Foreword

Written by Stevie Flood

Dear Readers,

Welcome to "Unveiling the Unrequited: A Journey Along Brandy Lane," a myriad of captured moments that delve deep into the intricacies of unrequited love—the timeless struggle of unfulfilled longing, unsaid words, and heartache that leaves a lasting imprint on the soul. In this poignant exploration of unrequited emotions, we embark on a path illuminated by the ethereal glow of Brandy Lane—a metaphorical lane that represents the emotional landscapes we traverse when faced with unreciprocated love.

Each page of this collection is a carefully crafted journey into the hearts and minds of individuals yearning for a love that remains elusive, either lost to time or never truly attained. Unrequited love is a powerful, universal experience that transcends boundaries and speaks to the core of human existence. Through these narratives, we aim to capture the colorful hues of this emotional spectrum—the joy, the pain, the acceptance, and the growth that stems from unreturned love. With authenticity as our compass, we present a collection of stories, poems, and reflections that mirror the diverse facets of unrequited love and resonate with readers from all walks of life.

Through the words penned on these pages, you are invited to reflect on your own experiences, empathize with the characters, and find solace in the realization that unrequited love is a part of the human experience, one that shapes us and, in its own way, makes us stronger.

Come, join us on this emotional expedition down Brandy Lane. Open your heart to the bittersweet tales that lie within and discover the beauty and resilience that often emerge from love unfulfilled.

With love and empathy,

Stevie Flood

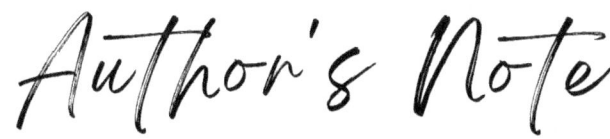

Author's Note

Thus, the angry poetry begins.

I was waking every day, wanting to do nothing but admonish you in light, but you decided to hide in the darkest caverns, barricading the way in.

Did loving me hurt too much? Or perhaps you never loved me at all? Maybe it was just some narcissistic game that you played. I don't want to believe that, but as you've said, "It was all in my head."

When did LOVE become a demon that I must wrestle with every day? One embrace that led to all-out war? My mornings are no longer "good"—the golden light has become an atrocity, a nuisance.

Love is like an addiction, and I am in the most severe of withdrawals. Funny, how what I thought was an act of giving was simply me getting high on your dimples when you used to smile.

Even Satan started as an angel, so I suppose it isn't too far-fetched that love—the one emotion that God himself called the greatest of all, could turn into something so painful, unwanted even.

Science has studied the effects of love on the human brain. Interestingly, being in love can cause the same issues as those suffering from narcissism and obsessive-compulsive disorder. I suppose I should've been institutionalized for my feelings for you. I guess I was truly crazy about you. I thought you felt the same. Perhaps your cure came sooner than mine.

Or, maybe it didn't. Maybe you needed to push me away because you also awaken tortured, and missing me. Maybe you realized that concupiscence is the name of the demon.

Unrequited

POETRY AND PROSE

Funny

Funny
how you thought
I was pretty.
I believed it
when you said it out loud.

I lived it.
I embraced it.

When I moved away,
I didn't hear it anymore.
I couldn't see it in your eyes,
and slowly...
your words grew cold
and as distant as I.

I swear...
I've aged twice as fast
in the absence
of your smile.

There's a heaviness
to my soul,
and happiness
is now a chore.

Funny
how it came so easily
in that one beautiful season...
the one in which
you loved me.

UNREQUITED

Too Late

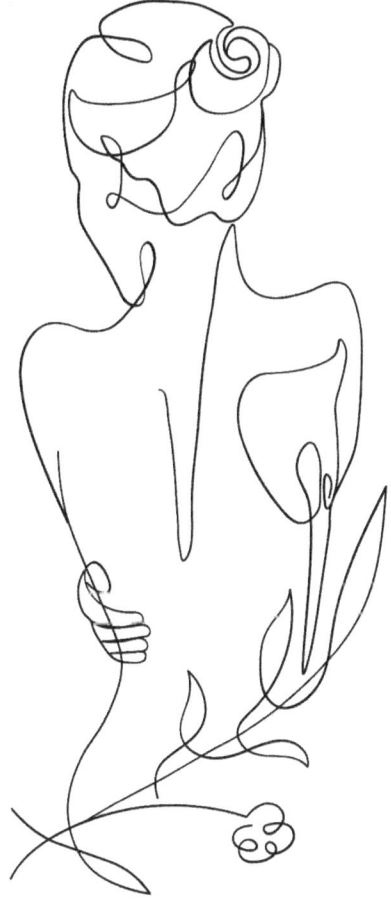

Please love, don't leave me!
Do not fade away!

Keep my heart in
scattered rhythm,
my breaths uncertain,
my hopes high.

Maintain my intoxication
to where flaws just fade away.

I beg of thee to allow
my remembrance
of his twinkling eyes,
the curvature of his mouth
when he laughs.

Do not deny me
the whispers,
as I still hear "I love you,"
echo in my head.

Forgive me—
for I recognized far too late,
he truly meant it.

Empty

I know you know,
that nothing has changed.

I still find comfort
in the memory of your touch,
your smile,
your laugh,
your compliments.
You, calling out my name—
although I cannot audibly hear—
constantly plays in my mind.

My feet still sweep the floor
searching for yours
to brush against.

My hands long for your
fingers, gently grazing mine.

Life is bland
and empty
without you.

Homeless

There are moments when
my soul crashes around
inside of my body.

It screams at me
and tells me that
I need to take it home.

I asked it,
"aren't you home inside of me?"
It replied,
"No, because you are not at home—
without him."

My Heart

My heart hurts,
it is so full of pain
that it makes my eyes leak
and takes my breath away.

My heart is barren...
I tried to fill it with ice cream,
I ate what was left of the pint...
but it still feels empty.

My heart is void...
like a black hole;
there is no gravity
keeping me grounded.

My heart is haunted
with the memories of you,
with woeful howls that echo
through its chambers.

My heart is weak...
I am somewhere
between life and death;
heaven nor hell
hold a home for me.

My home was with you,
but you left.

UNREQUITED

Say Goodbye

Love
is something
that I am certainly
no expert on.
I've been in it
and out of it.
I've fought for it,
and I've learned
when it was time
to let it go.

It most certainly hurts
when that time comes,
but if you truly,
unconditionally
love another person...
you won't be selfish
by trying to
keep them close
when you see
that it hurts them.

You will know
that the greatest
act of love
that you
can do for them,
is to thank them
for every beautiful,
wonderful moment—
and say goodbye.

All Alone

Close your eyes...

Can you feel my fingers
trace your hand?

Can you sense my smile,
content in your presence?

Can you feel my head
resting on your ample chest
as you breathe in and out?

My eyes searching for yours
as our fingers entwine?

I am right beside you.

I can feel you next to me...
even when I'm all alone.

UNREQUITED

Alive

What am I supposed to do?

I am in love with a dream
and if sleeping is the only way
that I can be with you,
then I will slumber for an eternity
just to feel you next to me.

That is when I come alive,
within my illusions at night.

Owned

You are right; I am owned.
I am owned by myself,
and have to answer to myself.

It may look as though
I made the wrong choice,
but my conscience is clear.

My heart chooses you.

Every single day I try to deny it—
unsuccessfully put it aside,
but it never fades, never dulls.

Trying to tell my heart
not to love you is like
denying a mother in labor
to birth her baby;
dreadfully painful,
and rather impossible.

I Refrain

Each moment that you see
a blank screen,
an empty inbox,
a quiet moment.

Know that it is my gift to you
painfully given out of love.
Because I want nothing more than
to fill your screen, to write you letters,
or call just to hear your voice—
but I refrain.

Not because I WANT to,
but to give you the time,
the space and the silence
that you so desire...

All because I love you.

Whole

You could vanish from this earth,
and I would still never be able to
get you out of my head.

Ever.

I could view every beautiful
person on the planet
and none would compare—
I would still wish it were you.

No laugh as wonderfully robust,
no eyes as deep and soulful,
no touch as soft, yet loving.

I could search my entire life,
over every crevice of the earth,
in every shadow,
and each ray of light—
and never will I feel
as whole
as when I'm with you.

UNREQUITED

To Be Held

I don't need to know
the weather outside,
because inside, I'm stormy;
the swirling turbulence
sends a chill down my spine.

My mind is in a fog,
my head in the clouds;
I search for warmth and comfort.
I think of you.

I wrap myself
in the memory of your smile,
and imagine your arms
wrapped around me.

The fog lifts,
the clouds dissipate,
the turbulence ceases.

I am left in the quiet stillness,
with your soul holding mine.

Soul Mate

I met my soul mate...

He's witty and charming,
loving and sweet.

He's genius-level at times,
(when he's not being his goofy self).

One minute, he's god-like, powerful...
the next, a playful kitten.

Mixed with utter brilliance,
is an air of cynicism.

He loves me deep down in his soul
I know he does,
(though he claims it's unrequited).

I recognized him the moment that I met him.
I dreamt of him immediately that night.
I dreamt we were toasting marshmallows
around a campfire, so innocent and sweet.

You must understand—
I wasn't looking.

I ran into him
like he was a cement barricade,
and I was going light speed.

UNREQUITED

You see, our souls have loved
for centuries... but this lifetime isn't fair!

This time around,
I found him too late,
or too early...
(I'm not entirely sure which),
because that "what if" lingers.

All I know is circumstances
are such that loving can hurt sometimes,
and timing does not allow for us
to be our true selves.

There is no doubt in my mind that he
is the one that my soul longs for.

But I cannot have him.

Most people will never understand
this kind of feeling, this depth of love—
it's on another plane altogether.

This love is not ephemeral,
it is the kind that never dies.
It may be dormant for a while,
but it will always be there.

Maybe in the next lifetime,
we will find each other again.

For now, I am trying to smother the fire
that burns within.
But every now and then—
a smoke ring escapes.

I Love You

I love you when there's coffee.
I love you when there's wine.
I just flipping love you
all of the freaking time.

I love you in the daytime.
I love you in the night,
and my heart doesn't care
if it's wrong or if it's right.

I'll love you every season,
whether Spring or mid-October!
I'll love you when I'm drunk
or while I'm stone-cold sober.

All I know is my heart
forever chooses you,
no matter if I'm happy,
or when I'm feeling blue.

I'll love you every day
until my very last,
for this love continues on
to the future, from the past.

If you haven't realized
how much I really care,
just look into my eyes,
but only if you dare.

War Cry of the Valkyrie

I can feel my heart beat again
for the first time in forever.
A different rhythm, like an old song
I'd forgotten the words to.
It strikes me as a welcome feeling,
but at the same time I'm glad
that I can't remember the words.
I'm happy that they are lost, forgotten—
because there's a reason the tune
lay silent now.

There's a reason
for my slight case of dementia.

All that remains is the rhythm.

It beats like the war cry of the Valkyrie—
a nervous pride swells up inside
and I swallow hard.
I know there are battles in my midst
that must be fought
before I can smile again.
I know there are losses to endure,
and more memories to be laid to rest.

Someday, I will come home again
with broken chains dangling from my wrists.
My face will bear a toothy grin amongst
tear-stained cheeks and crow's feet.

I will be home, and I will be free.

BRANDY LANE

All I ever Needed

All I ever needed was
a voice on the other side,
someone to give a gentle nudge
not there so much to guide.

Someone to share their thoughts
and not get mad if I object.
Someone to hear my secrets,
that I trust they will protect.

Someone to give me space
when they see it's sorely needed—
yet always there to listen,
whene'er I feel defeated.

I only needed you to be
the voice that echoed back
but louder and much stronger
with the courage that I lack.

After all, I am supposing—
that's what a mentor does.
A better confidant or friend
or muse there never was.

UNREQUITED

You'd chide me when 'twas needed,
whenever I'd cross the line,
then lovingly embrace me
and pour me a glass of wine.

We'd laugh and play and have such
fun until our eyes grew tired;
reluctantly, I'd let you go,
of course, hugs were required!

Oh, all I ever needed was
a soul that mirrored mine,
and I found that when I found you,
and it is so sublime.

I can only hope and pray,
(if they don't go unheeded)
that when I found you,
you found me too...
and I was all you ever needed.

Love has Flown

Love has flown,
there's no reason to smile here...
anymore.

Spread its wings with no warning,
not even a change in the atmosphere.

Ascended
without a farewell kiss.

I constantly look to the skies for a grand return,
to once again feel my heart trying to escape my chest...
but nothing comes.

Flurries fall and smash into my face,
melting with my tears;
the cold and the hot melting into a melancholy lukewarm.

Don't you feel my longing?
My soul screams for you as it is ripped in two.

I've half a heart and a mind-filled
with conversations that I could have sworn,
were true.

I suppose I must comfort myself,
for there are no wings
to wrap myself in.

I cannot help but wonder
if you are missing me too.

UNREQUITED

Loaded Gun

I fell in love with a dragon.
Of course, I should have known better—
when you play with fire, you get burned,
'specially with feelings unfettered.

I love him like no other man,
passions burning so deep within.
But, I suppose that concupiscence
is something quite equal to sin.

It was never my intention,
as my feelings were very pure,
and I was always so alone...
my marriage, so unsure.

I thought that I had a safety,
upon this cocked and loaded gun,
thought I could be a bit flirty,
and have a little fun...

And oh, it was... it really, really was.

I didn't know I'd fall in love,
I mean, I wasn't trying to.
But when that shot went off
it pierced our hearts,
and broke them right in two.

It still hasn't healed
and frankly,
I don't want it to.

If someone were to ask me about my life and what my favorite times were, those stories would include the few years that I got to spend with you.

Those are at the top of my list of happiest memories.

You know the kind— the ones where you smile, then cry.

Tell Me

Oh, how I long to hear you
tell me you love me.
That the words you used to whisper
were not just in my head.
I've loved you with a depth, inconceivable,
and to heights unreached by even
the most glorious airships
crafted by man.

I've loved you with a feeling of insanity
that I've been to countless professionals to cure.

They assure me I'm remarkable, fascinating,
and completely sane—
there is no cure for what ails me,
with one exception.

This feeling cannot stay imprisoned forever,
and I'm exhausted of keeping it locked away.
It's just not healthy to lie to myself every day,
keeping precious words unspoken.

You are still my heart's companion,
and this long pause is akin to death.

Just tell me again that you love me.
Tell me, and I am yours.

BRANDY LANE

Back Home

Chilly morning,
you put on a sweater,
pour out the coffee
and settle right down.
Ponder how you
could make your life better
and stay with your partner—
in that new town.

So many things change
in such a short time!
Your mind cannot fathom
what to do next.
Fresh out of a dream
of what could've been—
into reality,
feeling perplexed.

The past was great,
but we cannot dwell there,
let's keep the best parts
and move right along.
Different can be,
perhaps, even better...
than we could imagine,
what could go wrong?

I surmise there's just
one thing left to do
as I write down
this manuscript's ending—
that's to jot down an ellipsis
because it alludes...
to the future
that's constantly pending...

Walk with Me

Walk with me in the rays of sunlight
as the grasses shine with morning dew.
Hold my hand in the lingering glow—
remember fondly the love we knew.

Laugh with me like we did long ago
in the mid-life of our fading youth.
Hold me against your chest once again
to feel your heartbeat—its only truth.

Leaves hold the memories of our past—
brilliant, they turn in the light of day.
Before slowly dying, colors fade
and then, over time, meander away.

But the tree trunk still stands bare and tall,
ready to brace for the cold winter's storms—
anticipating the coming spring
when the sun's embrace is safe and warm.

My sweet love, I await your return,
with my arms outstretched, as the branches—
awaiting to bloom upon your touch,
into the sweetest of romances.

Moving On

Sorting,
cleaning out the junk drawer,
the closet...
trying to decide which parts of you
you want to keep
and what you want to toss away.

It's more than just changing location—
it's a time for mourning,
for nervous butterflies,
for goodbyes,
for new beginnings.

It is time to dust off the memories
with their tangible counterparts.
It is time to end a chapter,
to close a door for one last time.

It is time to move forward,
and take only the best of times
and place them in a box.

You know, the things that make you smile,
then reminisce because—
those moments may be gone,
but they are still so good
that you want to remember.
You want to hold on.

UNREQUITED

I know this is a hard time for you.
I know this is not what the plan was.
I know you are grieving inside.

I am here to remind you
that there is hope...
and you have people who love you,
that are cheering you on.

I don't care where you are,
you are still home to me,
and I will be right here
still loving you,
trying to make you smile...
and trying to console you
when you feel like
everything in the world
is against you.

I get that you are busy.
I hate that you have to go
through any of this.

More importantly,
I am hopeful that everything will work out
beyond your wildest dreams,
that you will find
more love, more success, and more joy
than you could ever dream.

My not-so-secret desire?

To see you truly happy again.

Empty House

Cardboard boxes filled with hope—
and memories not soon forgotten.
The light filters through the window
as transient dust lingers in the air.

Echoes of laughter
and ghosts of days past,
haunt one last time
in the bare-naked
chambers of this old house—
now still and empty,
hungry for more of the same.

There's a feeling inside of an empty house
that no one can put into words.
An ache, a finality, closure, uncertainty.
That feeling that you definitely forgot…
something.

This was where
I played footsie with you.
This was where you professed
you loved me.
This was where your fluffy companion
took his last breath in your arms.
This is where dreams began—
that are now on hold for a little while.
This is where you survived a pandemic.
This is where countless bottles of wine were shared.

This was home for at least a little while.

You created here, laughed here,
played here, flirted, slept, and had lovers here.

Don't worry, it wasn't the house
that caused it all to happen,
it was the essence—which is you.

Take all of the good,
leave what you want to behind—
and go forward with hope.

This is where I wish I could hug you
one last time at your door.

If you close your eyes, I am there.

One more, "I love you!"
whispered upon your chest.

Safe travels—I hope you find "home" again.

Lonely

I want to say something,
but I'm so afraid I'm overthinking
again.

Maybe nothing is wrong at all.
Maybe you are just busy—
taking a break from the buzz of the world.

What if you don't miss me?
Is that what I'm afraid of?
Maybe you'll wish you never
met me in the first place.

Part of me wants to say these things
and hear you respond with;

"Of course I miss you."
or "You have made my world a better place."

But your lack of response is more like a;

"If you can't say anything nice, don't say anything."

You already know I miss you every hour of every day.

Couldn't you yell at me or something?

UNREQUITED

Couldn't you tell me you don't want to see
or hear from me ever again?

At least then, I could be angry.

Because this feeling of not knowing
is worse than me just being able
to turn my love into hate.

*This waffling in the middle,
the gray area,
it is bleak and cold here—
and very lonely.*

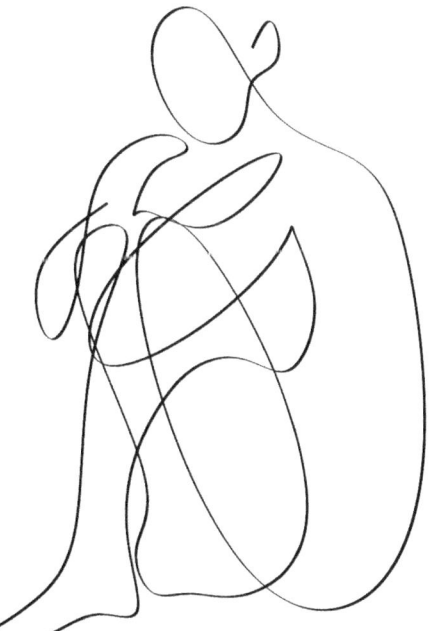

Bound

My tongue is bound
and I am in anguish—
filled with words that
I am no longer allowed to speak.

This punishment is unbearable to my soul
and I have no recompense to make amends.

I am not allowed to have feelings?
I have gathered that they are "wrong"
or "inappropriate" to have.

For ages, people have been fighting for their rights
to make their feelings known, and here I am—
marked with a scarlet letter
for something I haven't ever acted upon.

How can I help or hide the way I feel?
Why should I have to?
Why can I not have freedom
to have wild excursions in my mind?

Stories have been written for ages,
and I'm sure not all are only narrative.

I'd bet my life that most characters
are based on a mix of make-believe,
the grocer's hearty laugh,
the annoying next-door neighbor,
the overbearing husband, the jovial best friend,
or even a childhood pet.

UNREQUITED

People who know me,
know I live in a world in my head—
where I can hear
the plants and the animals around me conversing.
I carry on entire conversations
with the world around me.

My closest friends are usually in awe
when I narrate the animal's thoughts,
they say it seems believable.
Am I still waiting for the animals
to come and clean the house while I sing?

Yes.

Will I always feel trapped in a tower
as long as I'm not allowed—to freely express myself?

Yes.

Will I constantly make the guy
who was supposed to be My Prince Charming,
a now-evil character because of a horrible spell
that came over him—no matter how much
I want him to be better?

Probably.

Will I look at God as not just or fair,
since he has the power not to let these things happen—
but essentially, allowed them, ruining my happily ever after?

Most likely.

I'm constantly writing stories in my mind
and I have written myself into a place
where there are no easy answers.
I don't want to have to write off
a character by death—
nor do I wish to harm
the other characters.

However, the story cannot continue as it is.

Sweet and Hot

Are you my savior or my demise?

Are all of the sweet—yet torturous pains I feel
the only pleasure I can have in this life?

Like honey infused with a bite of habanero
there is a sweet pain that comes with knowing you.

You quench my thirst—
yet leave me parched at the same time.

I'm over-stimulated,
yet never want to stop—
even though I can't handle it anymore.

UNREQUITED

Yin and Yang

Maybe I avoided goodbye
because I wanted to
pretend that you could be mine
for just a little longer.

You made it clear
a long time ago
that it was him
or you.

I tried to keep you both
but not because
I felt the same
for either one of you.

Yin and Yang.
Cold and hot.

I was stuck in the middle
trying to find balance
and stay warm.

Then, I did the unthinkable—
I left without a proper goodbye.

Who does that?

Maybe it was because
I didn't think you would
give up so easily.

Maybe I thought you would follow me—
I hoped you would.

But, you didn't—or couldn't.
And I'm left cold and chaotic
inside my soul.

Don't you Fret

My darling, don't you fret—
it will come again someday.
That deep-seated joy
that seems to have escaped
from your bones.

Some days, it feels like the work is for naught.
The end of the day comes,
and the wine is the only thing to comfort you
and keep you warm.

Empty bottles add up, as do disappointments.
You play scratch-off lottery tickets
while praying for the big win,
but only finding a dollar here, a fiver there.

Melancholy has become a cloak to cuddle in—
and some days, the effort to smile—
is just too cumbersome, too painful.

Thinking of days gone by—
I wish for a time machine back to that feeling...

Thankful you had it,
yet not at the same time.

UNREQUITED

You want to erase it,
yet you hold on to it—
like a faded photograph
and tuck it into
the corner of your heart
for safekeeping—
as a tear escapes your eye.

Oh yes, my love...
it will come again,
and you will not be able
to tame it when it does.

It will enrapture you,
and lift you higher
than you ever thought possible.

That is always my wish for you.

BRANDY LANE

Spill

I have written *books* of poetry all about you.

I've surrounded myself with anything that I could—
that reminded me of you.

I memorized so many things;
the scar on your finger, your laugh,
the way you clear your throat,
your slight shuffle when you walk...

It is because I grew up being spoon-fed fairytales.
You know, the kind where if you wanted something enough,
it would inevitably come true.

Perhaps I am missing the magic spell, the fairy godmother—
because there is nothing that I've ever wanted more,
than to have your company.

I want the brushing toes, entwining fingers, and lingering hugs.
I crave the electricity I've only ever felt when we touched.
I desire the all-knowing glances and the meaningful gestures.

I don't want them from anyone that isn't you.

My happily-ever-after is only a fairytale, for now.
It is dripping in pretty pictures and woven words—
for others to FEEL even a moment
of the love I have, that fills my insides.

My love never fades, and I must keep it contained within
the covers that bind the pages of my heart—lest it spill out to the
world and cover it in hope.

Is it so terrible to have hope?
To wish that things would ever
work out in my favor?

UNREQUITED

I knew you When

I knew you when your eyes twinkled
and your laughter was joyous.

I knew you when
all I could see was love.

I wanted to breathe your air—
to see what you saw.
I wanted to feel what you felt,
and taste every bottle of wine
your lips touched.
I wanted to wrap myself
in your company.
I wanted you to envelop me
in your arms, in your soul, in your heart.

I am still in love with you...
and all of the things that I wanted,
are mere dreams now.

But it is only you
that I ever want to be that close to.
I want to come home,
but I'm so afraid that you
won't want me anymore.

My last "I love You"

Fading colors in my memories,
like death is looming,
but spirits remain.

Remembering your smile—
inevitably, my eyes crinkle,
then the corners of my mouth.

I still feel you next to me,
even though you are not here,
I ache for your hand to hold.

Oh, how I wish I hadn't fought fate!
I should've let the train go by
and stayed comfortably at home—
but I didn't.

I thought everything would be alright—
but it wasn't.
I'm left with a heart full of ache,
a mind full of regret,
and empty arms.

Lonely in a house
full of equally lonely people,
not knowing where they are headed,
and confused as to where they've been.

If I should die alone—
or perhaps in the arms of anyone else,
know that when I breathe my last,
it will be your face
that I am gazing upon in my mind...
and you will be my last "I love you."

UNREQUITED

Just in Case

In case my life's end is nearing—
I must proclaim your worth to me.

I know no not where or when my heart will cease,
but I do know that it always flutters whenever
time is kind enough to indulge me
with your company.

No earthly thing compares to the treasure,
I've found in our friendship.
My time here on earth grows shorter each day,
and my only regret is that
I am not in close proximity to you.

Whether smiling or in need of a hug,
I'll accept you either way.
I realize that my life's mission
since I found you,
is to stay.

I should've listened to my heart
and not my head,
because now my heart
is retaliating against me.

My health is deteriorating
because I ignored it.
My head is starting to realize—
that my heart was right.

I can go through the motions
for the rest of my life...
but it will be the death of me
to not have you.

Dying Embers

I'm so alone now that you're gone
I just don't want to carry on.
I'm just a half of what was whole,
an empty shell missing a soul.

The joy I have when you are near,
cannot survive on once a year,
the messages I've writ—unread,
the many things I wish you'd said.

It's like a death, but you're not dead,
there are still chapters in my head.

Maybe someday, our souls will heal,
we'll meet again and just be real.
Maybe again, the sparks will fly,
but as for now, let embers die.

Overwinter

I guess I should've learned
how to say goodbye
before everything turned sour.

I should've kept only
the most perfect moments
and left with them
before anything
had a chance to bruise them.

It's inevitable that leaves fall
and winter comes—
but I just wanted to hold on
to the spring and summer a little longer
while things were in full bloom.

I wonder if I tuck it all away for a while,
let it rest, let it overwinter—
if the buds will rise again
when spring comes—
if the roses will bloom once more?

Only time will tell—but for now,
I will try to stay warm
with the dying embers,
and the fading,
but still comforting memory,
of your smile.

BRANDY LANE

No Longer

I no longer want my favorite things;
no games, no wine, no more music to sing,
I don't care to wear my fancy dresses,
or do my makeup, or fix my tresses.

I won't listen to Gershwin anymore,
and writing poems has become a bore—
this, all because I no longer have you.
So now, pray tell, am I supposed to do?

The bright, glaring sun at the dawn of day?
Won't leave me alone— it won't go away.
I still say, "Good Morning!" but you don't care,
am I THAT much of a burden to bear?

People get sick of me and then run away.
I never know why—because they don't say.
Or can't. Or won't. I'm not sure the "what for,"
but it's quite impossible to ignore.

Not a friend in the world calls upon me—
no one wants to go get coffee or tea.
No friends ever pop by unexpected.
I feel lost, and utterly rejected.

UNREQUITED

I could vanish from Earth into thin air—
no one would miss me—they really don't care.
So I'll sit alone, crying at all that I've lost.
I would do anything—no matter the cost—
to be as close as we were—to make amends
to laugh, and sing, and play as friends!

I'd give anything to look into your eyes
again, without a mask, sans all disguise...

To love you unabashedly,
to experience that frivolity,
to get dolled up again in pretty dresses,
to blush my cheeks and comb my tresses.

To drink and lose our breath in laughter,
in your eyes see, happily ever after,
to embrace feeling the electricity—
that had for you and you had for me.

What's the Point?

What's the point in good mornings
when there's no good to be had?

The sun is shining,
the birds are chirping
and I'm just downright sad.

I used to look forward to getting up
and chatting throughout our days—
but then you just stopped responding,
told me to go away.

All of my paints are peeling—
all the pictures you helped me to make.
All of that work, the hours I spent,
were they wasted, for goodness sake?

I'm confused,

I thought you were my friend.

"You're my family!"

I must've done something really wrong
to make you want to leave.

UNREQUITED

Now I'm just here crying,
all I can think of is you—
which is the exact opposite
of what I'm supposed to do.

All of the love poured out—
like diamonds tossed into the sea.

The tears dripped down,
their silent plea
for the love you no longer
have for me.

Yours

All this time, I was looking for you...
but you've been here all along.

I was blinded and could not see!

Oh, how hard it must have been!
Me, in the shadows, crying out for you...
You, right there, telling me everything will be alright,
but in the chaos, I was deafened.

No wonder you turned your head away—
what a helpless feeling it must've been.

Don't fret, my mind is coming back,
now that the doldrums have passed.

When I could not share my mind
you allowed me your hand to hold.

You let me snuggle by your side
when you knew I needed you most—
but could not speak the words to ask.

I'd lost my will, which started to affect my mind...

UNREQUITED

But my darling,
I want you to know
that all the thorns that were growing—
were not to keep you out.

No, they were to protect my heart
that was blooming for you.

They were there to keep others
from damaging
the one worthy thing
that I have left.

*They can take my mind and my body—
But, my heart they cannot have,
for that part is yours.*

BRANDY LANE

Obsession

Here I am in the quiet—
screaming on paper again.
Ink bleeding into the dried pulp of a tree.
I know you hear me, but you won't come.

It must have been tiring to watch,
because you didn't want me
to love you anymore.

You called it an obsession,
an infatuation.
You whiplashed me
to the other extreme—
like a slap in the face
that I didn't deserve.

Now I'm alone,
wounded in this ravaged body.
I want the one person
that I thought would always stay
to come and hold me again.

I know why you backed away;
because you couldn't bear
to watch me in agony.

I'm not even mad—
I just miss you.

UNREQUITED

Where is the Joy?

Where is the joy I brought you?
Did you give it all away?
Is it tucked behind a chair,
for, perhaps, another day?

Where are the silly anecdotes
you used to share with me?
is the laughter that we shared
now, just history?

What happened to your love?
Did it vanish in thin air?
Because now when I reach out,
You're barely even there.

I know that people change,
But I will still love you,
that is... unless you feel
that you don't want me to.

Intoxicate

I cannot help that I am in love—
it is like a disease I cannot eradicate.
But there's a loveliness in the sorrow that does not fade—
like the gloomy comfort of the rains in the spring.

Hope springs forth and blooms in the gardens of my inner depths.
The fragrance of my love for you intoxicates my mind,
everything becomes soft and glorious.

It has imbued every molecule of my existence,
and played the strings of my heart so finely—
that any measure of music resonates through my core,
releasing a high that cannot be replicated.

No wine, no drug, just you.

Flesh and Bones

Don't you know that I want your flesh and bones, love?

No more metaphors, no more poetry.

Just your broken and bruised heart,
so I can caress it in my hands
and heal you bit by bit?

I want your burdens, your tears, your grief to bear.
Not because you are all of these things I've written for you...
but because you are real.

I want you.
Not in a fantastical, happily-ever-after kind of way.
I want you in the ways that I can care for you tangibly—
to cry with you when you are sad.

I want to meet you on the ground,
fallen in the dirt and torments of life—
and hold you.

I want you to feel held, loved, whole.

I've never wanted to run to anyone so much
as I want to run to you.

Ache

It's the middle of the night,
a mere two hours before dawn,
and all I want to do is tell you
how much I love you.

Alas, I cannot—
for you asked me not to.

You gave my heart back to me,
even though, I know you love me too.

It was the chivalrous thing to do.

But you see, there's a problem;
my heart hasn't been beating right
since you returned it,
and now—there's this horrible pain in my chest
that causes my eyes to leak.
I can't sleep,
and it seems to have affected
the smile on my face.

Yes, I know we're still friends—
the best,
and I know you aren't leaving me
in that capacity.

But when I gave you my heart
for safekeeping—
I think you might
have accidentally
broken it.

UNREQUITED

All of a sudden,
my dreams are gone,
and my poems have no rhyme.

There's no magic
or fairy dust
in my world,
it's just...
gone.

I missed you before
I knew you even existed,
and I miss you more now
that you're here.

I am not going to pretend
that I understand
why God allows
these things to happen
but...

I'd still rather
have this ache in my chest
than the nothing
that was there before.

My Love in Ruins

You broke down my walls,
my fortress in ruins,
and now, the light and rain
do what they will.

Ivy runs through the spaces
of the well-placed cornerstone,
the foundation with which
our friendship is built.

Flowers bloom now
where shadows once resided...
around the stones that represent
the not-so-distant past.

Our love, but a whisper on the wind...
whistles through the spaces
now clear of mud and mortar—
sharing stories, never to be lost.

UNREQUITED

Ruined

Why do memories have to fade—
leaving echoes
where boisterous laughter
and shenanigans used to be?

I wish there was a portal
I could step into—
back to the innocence,
back to the feelings
that washed over me, afresh
each time I would see you.

We were grasping at
our quickly disappearing youth,
drinking and flirting
like tomorrow would never come—
as though we were immortal.

I worshipped you,
adored you,
loved you,
and you loved me—
at least for a moment.

I have never been happier
than in that year that you loved me,
and I fear that I will never
feel that way ever again
for anyone.

You've ruined me for everyone else.

Nothing Compares

You were my drug of choice...
I was higher than a kite whenever you would cross my mind—and I could never overdose... you just made me so happy, so comfortable, so contented. Nothing in the world compares!

But you quit being my supplier.
I'm not sure if you were slowly running out of the sweet candy your looks supplied—or if you were weaning me off because you felt it was the right thing to do—
but you've left me wanting...

The laughter.
The banter.
The soul-baring glances
The companionship.
The warmth.
The compliments.
Oh, those sweet compliments...

I'm going through withdrawal.
Nothing can take the place of you...
No other.
No liquor.
No drug.

Nothing compares to the way you've made me feel.

UNREQUITED

It's Over

It's over.
I had finally found joy...
but it's over.

He's gone.
Sentiments grown cloy...
but he's gone.

I thought for a moment
ever so fleeting
that he'd be mine.

BRANDY LANE

Words

As I sit in an old ballroom,
poring over books of all kinds,
I ponder that I am surrounded
by thousands and thousands of words.
Yet,, none hold any depth to me—

for they were not born from your lips.

UNREQUITED

I Will Never be Fine

I am living a lie, falling apart...
I'm not really here—just playing the part.
Always surrounded, forever alone
even with family inside of my home.

I saw a beacon—in darkness, it came
followed that light like a moth to a flame.
My soul was at peace—it basked in the light,
of his gentle smile on that lovely night.

I was often abused and neglected...
yet with him, I was always respected.
I admittedly fell, and I fell hard,
for that musician, that writer, that bard.

But stories and dreams must now come to an end,
I've a family to raise, so we're just friends.
But oh, what wonderful mem'ries I'll take—
the rest of my days—my love, I'll forsake.

The circumstances just did not align.
Part of me feels I will never be fine...

No, I will never be fine— without him.

Never

I have concluded—
that I will never be happy in love.
I will never taste true love's kiss.
I will miss out on the tangible caresses
and holds, the sweet breath of your soul
pouring into me.

I shall never know what it is like
to hold your hand in mine,
to walk along the pathway
into the sunset.
It was all just a beautiful dream—
a fairy tale romance
that I wrote in my mind.

You played the part perfectly,
chivalrous and kind.

You played the part so well
that I fell head over heels in love with you.
I forgot you were just a character—
a muse,
someone to use...
while I was falling apart inside.

UNREQUITED

She realized that she had mistook being needed for being loved—and that those, altogether, are two vastly different things.

She had settled for what was right in front of her instead of everything she ever wanted.

Don't Pray for Me

Don't pray for me
I beg of thee—
I've already made my confession.
I shall wear my scarlet letter proudly,
just because I can.

I have no reason to hide
the love I have inside,
because it is untainted,
pure like virgin snow.

The purest love you'll ever know.

Judge me all you want,
I really don't give a damn,
fact is that I never betrayed anyone.
I never denied love—just urges,
never the mind, heart, or soul...
just the body.

Unconditional love, ahh yes,
isn't that what we are called for?
To love?

So, I love him.
I love him.

Oh, how I love him.

UNREQUITED

Don't pray for me,

I have already made it to heaven,

I have already felt the hand of God,
seen forever in the eyes
of the earthbound angel.

I don't need to straighten my halo.

Sweet perfection in his glances,
his words,
his milky voice.

He loved me once,
not too long ago.

And that is all I need to know.

Almost Love

We flirted—nonchalantly—
because we knew it could never happen.

But nothing could've prepared me
for how my heart wanted it to.

My soul followed, then my brain,
all the while telling me it was all
just make-believe—
but it wasn't.

We never crossed the threshold,
never invaded that territory—
as though it were riddled with landmines.

There we were—almost wanting, almost craving,
almost kissing, almost touching.

Almost…

I will never be satisfied with that.

I've wanted to finish what we started
from the moment we laid eyes on each other.

I want to taste your mouth on mine—
crave your fingertips on my flesh,
embrace you as though we are soul to soul.

But I'm trapped in "almost,"
and I suppose that is better than "never,"
but I don't want to end at "not quite"—
when I was hoping for "forever."

UNREQUITED

Oh, there is no denying that there is love here,
but for all intents and purposes...
for the time being, "almost" will have to do.

Although, in my dreams, we've already had
mind-blowing interludes—
and long walks at sunset while holding hands.

We've snuggled under blankets,
sharing bottles of wine and popcorn
as we watched movies—
while our hands playfully wandered
beyond the bowl.

We've sat at the breakfast table over coffee,
eyeing one another, grinning,
and trying to discipline ourselves to get to work.

I've always felt like ink
trying to separate myself
from the fibers of the paper I was drawn on
when it comes to leaving you.

This "almost love" has been better
than any other love, I've known...

Almost.

I Simply Love You

To know for a brief moment, or even a short while,
amongst the sea of chiseled faces and beautiful derriere's,
I held your gaze long enough to know you loved me.
Even though fleeting, it pierced my heart for eternity.
No one will ever see me as you did.

To know that even though I will never be your cup of tea,
you played the Mad Hatter to appease my inner Alice.
We played rounds of Hearts
while we painted our palates red with wine.
I feasted on your compliments—
that never made me feel smaller, only perfectly adequate.

I knew that even though I wasn't what you expected—
what you knew you never wanted,
you still cherished and loved me to the very core.
I know because I felt the same.
Perfectly imperfect, unconditional love.
That hasn't changed, for you still are my favorite dream.
Pinch me!
No, wait... just a few more moments before I must awake.
I don't wish to wake up from the days of chatter and song,
of red lips and pretty dresses— of you in all colors of blue
that bring the oceans in your eyes alive.

I don't want the feasts, games, or silly banter to fade... just yet.
I have said it before,

"I never knew I needed you, and now I don't ever wish to be without."

I think you must not believe me—but it's true.
You are part of me now, a part that I would be broken without.
You are beautiful and magical and a transformative part of my life.

And I simply... Love you.

UNREQUITED

Thinking of You

I was eating little potatoes with Herbs de Provence
and thought of you ('cause it's French).

I opened a beer and thought of you
and how you are not a beer person—
how generously you pour the wine,
and how the beer will never measure up.

I listened to someone read my poem online
and thought of you because I miss you so much.
If you were anywhere near,
maybe my heart would calm,
and I could see what the world looks like
when it's not in watercolors.

I looked out the window and thought of you
in the pitch black of night.
I felt so small while thinking
of how tiny my love must seem from far away.
Up close, it's like a giant fireball
that can never be dimmed,
and although it sparkles like a diamond—
from that distance, you can no longer feel its heat.

I hugged my blanket and thought of you
and how much I desperately need you in my life.
How I never quite felt alive until you existed in my world,
and how every day I wake up excited to know you.

Dragon wings envelop me,
as I imagine your arms around me.

I wrote this, all while still thinking of you.

BRANDY LANE

Fallen

Don't leave me, I beseech you.
Don't go, please, I implore!
I beg of you to stay with me—
just for forevermore.

I don't want you to go yet,
I'd love for you to stay,
not just for a moment, but—
for always and a day.

I have to have you near me,
you just cannot depart—
for if you were to go away
now, that would break my heart.

You see, I start to miss you
the moment that you leave—
as soon as your car leaves the drive
that's when I start to grieve.

I don't want to feel this way
but, dammit, I just do...
If I am being honest-
I've fallen hard for you.

UNREQUITED

I Already Know

I'm afraid to try again...
because it might hurt.

I'm still trying to argue in my head
whether you betrayed me on purpose
or whether my
PERCEPTION
caused me to feel that way...

Either way, I'm timid...
like a turtle in its shell.

How can we be carefree again,
like we were before?

Is it over?

That ONE question
is more frightening to me
than anything else.

I don't want to know
but I need to know...
or maybe...

I already know.

Never Again

If you were to decide to never speak to me again, it would be a pain worse than death.
You not caring anymore would be something I could never come to terms with—because not hearing your laughter or feeling your warmth against my skin is punishment enough.
I would not want to exist in a world you were no longer a part of.

Because... never again would I see your face,
or feel the warmth in your embrace.

Never again would there be chatter,
discussing all of the things that matter.

Never again would I hear your voice,
I wouldn't even have a choice!

You would be missing, but I'd be here.
I'd mourn you with every tear.

I would think of you every now and then,
but I would not get to see you—
ever again.

*It just hit me—
we love each other,
we are just on pause...*

Love Isn't Enough

I love you, but love isn't enough—
to keep you.

Oh, I imagined all of the things we
would've done together—

If only...

But even though the love is there,
nothing else is.

You saw that long ago,
but I didn't want to accept it.

People have said, "All you need is love."
No, you also need
understanding,
patience,
kindness,
and to be content within yourself.

You also need a roof over your head,
and in this world—
a way to make a living.

I cannot love you like I want to,
and I fear the feeling is mutual—

But...

Why does it have to hurt so much—
watching you walk away?

In Your Arms

I do not need to be in the same house as you, the same town as you, the same state, country, or continent as you.

I feel your presence even when you are crossing the oceans—vast and far away.

How do you expect me to be on the same planet as you, breathing the same bitter air, and not be thoroughly in love with everything you are?

The world could be engulfed in flames, the birds all drop from the sky, the oceans could dry up, and everything could wither—but the thought of the moments when you loved me, even in their brevity, would keep me breathing—would keep me searching for you.

Armageddon could sweep us off of the face of the earth, and if I couldn't find you in the heavens—I would beg to be cast down to hell just to be with you again.

My soul will never be content until I am once again in your arms.

I Want to be Kissed

Nope. I don't ever want to be owned again.
Never, never, never.

I want to love unabashedly and be kissed like he needs me to exist. I want to have complete and undeniable trust and passion. I don't want any barriers—no reason to doubt anything he says or does. I want to be completely loved and without any doubt or anger.

I want him to look at me as though I am the epitome of everything he's ever desired—like I am priceless and worthy. I want to reciprocate without hesitation—his lips upon mine, our breaths in sync.

I want to love him like he's the only cure for my aching chest, my longing soul, my tired body.
I want to come alive within the magic of his words as he whispers in unbelief at his good fortune—to finally have me in his arms.

I want more than to just be wanted...

I want to be loved unconditionally, passionately, and demonstratively.

I want to be kissed like I'm a privilege to be with—not a prize to be won.

UNREQUITED

Unbroken

Reign me back in,
for I've grown
unruly and wild—
a morose
and a rather
melancholy child.

Take me back
to the longing,
the wanting of you—
as my eyes flit
from your lips
to your eyes, so blue.

Tell me words
I need to hear
loudly spoken—
the ones
that will keep
my fragile heart,
unbroken.

Queen of My Dreams

In the gauzy haze of dreams,
where memories saunter through your mind,
do you ever catch yourself in a soft smile—
and realize you are thinking of me?

I see you in the smoke,
and realize my heart is still ablaze.

I have been through the war,
and have come to terms with the fact
that I've been fighting for the wrong captain.

I should've gone rogue and fought for myself.

I am the queen of my dreams—
it is up to me to make them a reality.

I am Cassandra

From heavy mist
the memory of myth
Is from where I am summoned.

Time oozes liquid crystal
fallen from stars' realms
where the universe is the future.

Constantly trapped are we
in the light from yesteryear,
as we spin from dawn to nightfall.

I am more than this.
You are more than this.
We are more than this.

I got wrapped up in the gravity
for a moment—forgetting who
I am supposed to be.

I am an ethereal being,
Flitting through time
trying to find you as you roam—

in search of me.

BRANDY LANE

Alien

Midnight blue hues surround me in the quiet
as a lone cricket plays his violin.
I see the stars flicker in the vastness beyond—
light years from where they began.

I oft wonder if we're only echoes from before...
images like a hologram.
Or if we're tangibly in place yet, the universe fills us
with emotions deep within.

All I know is my gravity shifted the moment
you entered my atmosphere—everything within the
cosmos of my mind, the galaxies of my soul,
my heart's moon changed when you came near.

Like a comet racing through the sky,
you collided with my intrinsically placed satellites—
dashed through my stratosphere in a blaze,
and crashed into my most remote island.

My terrain irrevocably changed—
your alien ways infected my earthen crust
and wrenched deep caverns upon
your haphazard impact.
I'm left, gasping for oxygen, for gravity.

I slink inward, afraid of what all of this means.
Unaware of what lies within.
Extrovert becomes introvert as the dark
becomes my only friend.

My mind—a danger to itself.

UNREQUITED

The being in love part of it all...
the muse—

I can separate.

I can burn all of the books,
unpublish my pages,
erase all of my hard drives...

I would, if it meant that you
would be my friend again.

YOU are the important part,
NOT words that I have written.

The words mean absolutely nothing
without you in my life—
they practically erase themselves
from the pages.

There is no point,
when you were at the pinnacle.

No need for a pedestal
as the statue has up and disappeared.

No reason for a museum,
without any masterpieces to gaze at.

Empty pages to match my empty heart,
all because you decided I was no longer
your minstrel.

Loving a Ghost

The days trudge on by,
the pain never dulls.
My heart used to skip,
but now it just lulls.

I fight not to write
good morning to you
Instead, I now cry.
You don't have a clue.

I thought you loved me!
I guess I was wrong—
I should've known better,
that It wouldn't last long.

But all of the words
I've written to you,
are bound to my soul,
each one of them true.

I cannot erase you
you're too much a part—
of my thoughts, my prayers,
my now-broken heart.

It wasn't a thought
I'd lose you this soon—
you just disappeared,
that one afternoon.

UNREQUITED

Left without warning,
with nary a trace.
Too much of a coward
to speak to my face.

The door, when left open...
lets in the cold draft,
Where there once was warmth
as we played and laughed.

I struggle to close it
in case you come back—
but fear that you won't,
my confidence lacks

Are you waiting for me
to shut tight the door?
Do you truly not—
love me anymore?

You were the one friend
that I loved the most,
but it's really lonely—
loving a ghost.

BRANDY LANE

Into my Soul

Eyelids closed, still dreaming.
Your lips press against my forehead—
then my cheek.

You look into my eyes,
our heads touching at our hairlines,
all I see is blue as I feel the warmth of your love
seep through my body—
and into my soul.

First Kiss

If I could turn the tables
go back in time...
I would have the power
to place myself within your grasp.

What if I was your first kiss?

Your only kiss?

The only one you ever wanted.

BRANDY LANE

Dismay

My heart let go of love today—
it had to leave—it couldn't stay.
No explanation to relay...
just turned his back and walked away.

I guess one thing I must convey,
my tattered heart, now on display—
still beating, but in an erred array...
never thought it'd happen this way—

Or ever, much to my dismay.

UNREQUITED

Does God Write Poetry?

When God was done with Earth and Sky,
with things that swim and things that fly,
He looked down from his throne on high—
and pondered, then let out a sigh...

His breath formed into clouds that lay
around your forehead, streaked with gray,
that turns to silver, in sun's ray—
makes you dashing, I must say.

He's added lines over the years,
some formed from smiles, some from tears,
some from sleepless nights from fears—
that rumble round between those ears.

Oh, I've seen the poetry of God's pen
and how he edits again, and again,
forms changing ev'ry now and then
for everyone since life began.

Your stanzas I have memorized,
they are most beautiful, I won't lie.
So, I'll embrace them by and by
and recite them till the day I die.

BRANDY LANE

My Love

My love transcends the heights and depths,
the shadowed corners, and the breadths
of anywhere that you may be,
a mountaintop, valley, or sea.

It finds you in the vast abyss
when everything's askew, amiss,
and pulls you back through space and time,
brings back the rhythm and the rhyme.

My lofty thoughts of trees and sky
and of the birds in clouds so high
float aimlessly in search of you,
amongst the atmosphere of blue.

They soar to heights not yet been flown,
a love so rare—no one has known,
up where the crystals form, then fall
to kiss the cheeks of one and all.

I pray one lands upon your face,
with such a soft and gentle grace,
that you can feel the warmth of me,
within that icy filigree.

And as it melts upon your flesh,
your soul will feel renewed, refreshed…
absorbing deep into your skin,
migrating to your heart, within.

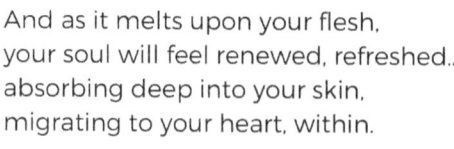

UNREQUITED

Adorned in You

There are days when
I want to wear a pretty dress—
the kind that makes me feel
a little more elegant,
and not so clumsy.

Sometimes, I decide on the leggings with the
baggy sweatshirt... for that bit of comfort
that I so desperately desire.

Then, there are the moments
where all I want to wear—is you,
for you give me all of the best comforts,
while still allowing me to feel that elegance.

The feel of you on my skin is of the rarest silk.
Your words douse me in sweet perfume.
Your breath is as feathers, tickling my flesh.

Your warmth fills me within my cold bones.
Your love completes my shattered heart,
and your essence fills my soul.

I want to be adorned in you every day.

Dream of You

In the hush of this morning
the only sound I hear
is the dull tinkling
of tiny ice shards
tapping at my window pane.

It seems they want to come in, too.

My bed is cozy, and
I slept well, although
never enough
to want to leave
the warmth my body created.

It seems I'm a regular furnace!

Vision blurred, and
ears still ringing,
mouth dry and tummy
grumbling. I snuggle
deeper into my cocoon.

And decide to dream of you a little longer.

Never Just a Muse

You were never just a muse to me,
no, that was just my excuse to write to you
to let you know how beautiful you are.

That was my disguise to be able to share my
feelings with the world. My own version of
Cyrano De Bergerac, but instead of me hiding
behind a mask, I gave you a cover.

I cloaked you whilst bragging about you.
I shined because of the words I wrote for you.
They weren't meant for me...
they were really only meant for you.

You are my pen. You are my heart.
You—are the reason I can feel again,
the reason I go on every day of this life.
You are the reason
I want to awaken every day.
You are my joy, even if it is bittersweet.

I keep hoping the stars will align,
wondering how I could've missed my comet—
patiently hoping for its return.

Knowing my love is on this earth,
and so many things are keeping me from you—
I know it is some twisted fate, and that at some
point, in some realm,
we were star-crossed lovers.
Because when I look at the night sky,
all I see is you—looking back at me.

Our love spurned galaxies—once upon a time,
to remind us of who we are.

The Rabbit

I'm like the rabbit in her den,
awaiting the spring's return.
I feel my heartbeat, breath in sync,
but oh, how my soul doth yearn.

The want is great although the needs
have been met throughout this time.
The freshness of new grass and weeds
would be utterly sublime!

The warmth of Sol is shining down
upon my soft, downy fur,
chasing away the cold and damp,
sleepy life begins to stir!

Much like the rabbit, I await
a day when my love returns,
for though he is so far away,
he's everything my soul yearns.

Contented

I'd be contented
wrapped in your arms,
breathing the same air
that has passed through your lungs.

I'd be honored
to be in your presence,
Just enthralled by simply
staring into your eyes.

I'd be thankful
for every moment,
treasuring the milliseconds
as though they are rare.

Chosen Family

Smiling faces all around
but none of them quite right
I'd rather yours, even when frowned
to get me through this night.

I don't need perfect smiles
getting along amicably...
what I need
are the beautiful flaws
of my CHOSEN family.

Pieces of Me

You take a little here, a little there...
My poetry, my recipes, my joy.

You use my energy, my peace,
My love, my time...

I gave them freely,
only to be left with nothing...
because you acted without
reciprocating...

Just like everyone else.

Nothing else satiates
this palate of mine.
One laugh, one smile,
one soul...

That is all I desire.

UNREQUITED

Dream

Last night, I had a glorious dream
that you came by to visit me,
I gifted you with dress-up clothes,
lots of kisses and letters of prose…

You donned the outfit at first sight
without even putting up a fight!
My God! You looked just like Voltaire—
from neck cravat to derrière!

I planted a kiss right on your face
as we collapsed in an embrace.
I must've passed out in a swoon
for I awoke as the "little spoon!"

Oh, how glorious just being with you,
even if for only an hour or two.
It's the only place where I can be
alone with you—just you and me.

BRANDY LANE

Already Yours

There is no sight I long for more
than your eyes gazing into mine.
No sound sweeter than when
you roll my name from your lips.

No feeling better than
being cozied up next to you on a couch
or in a warm embrace.

No moment has gone by
that I'm not wishing you were near—
not since the day we met.

You are so much more
than I could ever dream
a man could hold within his heart and soul.

You have so much inside of you
but are so restrained.

Still so chivalrous,
keeping me out of trouble—

*because you know my soul
is already yours.*

Just One More

"Just one more" of everything
is all I'll ever need.
Just one more game, one more hug,
just one more poem to read.

It's not that I am greedy,
it's just I love you so,
"one more day of everything"
I'd like before you go.

Just one more conversation,
to gaze upon your face.
Just one more chance to hold you close,
in a warm embrace.

Just one more meal to feast on,
one more cheesecake to bake.
Just one more laugh with you before
I, my last breath, take.

BRANDY LANE

She Really Loves You

She left me for a little while.
I missed her so very much—
the me that I knew when I was with you.

I didn't think she'd come back,
I felt so alone most of the time,
but she was lurking, remembering.

The way her toes would brush against yours.
The way your fingers entwined.
The way she stared into your eyes,
and didn't want to ever stop.

She knew it was all wrong and all right—
and everything that mattered all at once.

She loved you as no one could fathom.

She loves you.

Man, she really loves you.

Stranded

You were my island, my oasis, my dream—
the place I go when I want to feel at home.

You were my remedy for all that ails me,
my serotonin high, and my dopamine comfort.

Lately, I feel stranded, thirsty, exhausted, and
altogether homeless.

Wardrobe

Fingering clothes in my wardrobe,
and their intentions on my flesh;
I ponder each of their contents,
polyester, cotton, or mesh.

I then contemplate the weather,
whether it's rainy, hot, or cold;
and make decisions based on if
it makes me look too young or old.

I caught a glimpse of a fabric,
peeking carefully through the rest—
didn't used to be a favorite,
but now it is one of my best.

It's not because of its color,
its pattern, or the way that it fits,
or that it's very glamorous,
(It isn't) not one single bit.

UNREQUITED

I chose it just because it is
a rare one of the very few
I actually own from the days
that I used to spend time with you.

It helps me fondly remember,
my very happiest of days—
the way I'd get tingly inside
whenever your eyes met my gaze.

I wear it now as a symbol
of who I desire to be—
who I become when I'm with you,
is my favorite version of me..

BRANDY LANE

Guilt

Beautiful things
that once brought joy
are tainted now;
with streaks of disdain
and dusty salt
from dried-up tears.

Behind bars of regret
guilt has become
a prison cell.
Secrets hidden
deep within
locked away.

UNREQUITED

The Day I Met You

The shirt wasn't what I was after.
No, it was the way it brought attention
to those sapphire eyes.
Perhaps it was the way you rolled up those sleeves,
showing off those brawny arms—
or the way it set off the silver in your hair.

It may have been the tiny tuft
that would fluff out the top of your shirt on occasion,
or maybe it was the way it had me imagining you
in the Canadian wilderness—planting trees
and roasting marshmallows around a campfire.

I wore a gingham dress when I was little, it was blue—
just like your shirt. It was my absolute favorite.
You, dressed in blue gingham,
often made me think of us as children—
or how we close would have been had we known one
another "back in the day".

I often wish I'd gotten to know you sooner,
and the feeling remains that I knew you in prior lives,
different eras, multiple centuries.
I've never been able to shake that feeling,
nor do I want to.
All I know is that I have never felt this way for another.

The day I met you,
is the day my world gained color,
and I don't ever want to see
in black and white again.

Like an Addict

I'm sitting here
like an addict.
I took Facebook and Messenger off
of my phone today.

Why?
Because I kept looking for him.

I need to give him space!
He's not mine to keep track of.
I'm not his mother
or his sister
or his wife.
I'm his friend.

I love him, and I refuse to be selfish.
I want him to be happy.
So, I am setting myself free from worry.

In doing that...
I am setting him free to love me on his terms...

whatever that looks like.

Why am I still sitting here...
like an addict?

I've loved deeply, passionately, romantically, blissfully, lustfully — I've loved so much that I could feel the other person's pain, their joy...

and when they no longer loved me.

Bittersweet

This love I have is bittersweet,
such as fine chocolate or deep red wine—
or Autumn's bold burst of colors,
as leaves die off for the wintertime.

Final moments with a loved one
as they breathed their very last—
reminiscing laughter and love
from a not-so-distant past.

I'll savor every sip and bite,
as though it is a rarity—
as I live my life every day
with a new all-knowing clarity.

Think of Me

Do you ever think of me
in the quiet when I'm not there?
Do you ever miss my laugh,
My perfume in the air?

Do you wonder what I'm up to
when you don't hear from me...
or if today I'm having coffee,
or drinking some hot tea?

Do you ever reminisce
over moments that we've shared
letters written back and forth,
showing that we cared?

Because sitting here in the quiet,
that's all I can do,
is wonder if you think of me
as oft as I think of you.

A glimpse of
existential ecstasy
exists in your eyes.

I fall into your
charismatic chaos
quite comfortably.

UNREQUITED

You Are All I See

When I close my eyes,
you are all I see.

Your face is mere inches from mine
as we stare into the depths
of one another.

My heart beats fiercely,
my breath is stuck between
panting and being held,
my nose touches yours—
then our foreheads,
we turn and are cheek to cheek.

My hands find yours
and our fingers entwine.
Our mouths hovering
next to one another—
breathing in each other's exhalations.

It's as if I'm getting high
on your very soul!
We bask in the ecstasy
of each other's essence,
our breathing syncs as if we are one.

Our faces turn, nose to nose again,
our eyes half closed,
am I dreaming?

Our lips accidentally touch,
and a shock goes to my toes,
you must've felt it in kind
and your lips press firmly into mine.

I let out a little moan…
and much too soon—
wake myself up.

Oxygen

If I went missing...
would you come find me?
Would you look until
you knew
what happened to me?

Or would you just figure that life
had just carried me away—
like a fallen leaf in a
rapid stream.

Would you say goodbye,
or would you carry me in your bones
until your lungs
no longer breathe oxygen?

Starved

My mouth waters
sometimes
when I think of you.

It's a thirst
trying to quench itself...

Just a little taste
of those succulent lips.

A craving
that makes my brow lift
& my nose twitch.

Just one little taste?

I bite my lip
with no satisfaction.

I'm left,

STARVED.

BRANDY LANE

Without Fail

Every single day, without fail...
I imagine what it will feel like
when I see you again.

The funny thing is,
it's the same way I felt
when I'd see you often;
weak in the knees, breathless,
heart palpitating, nervous,
and the happiest I'd ever been.

I think about you always,
and it always makes me feel
like I've visited home,
even if only for a brief moment.

UNREQUITED

The Corner

Please tell me there's a corner,
tucked somewhere in your mind...
that we are cuddled closely,
somewhere no one can find.

I also have that corner,
that's where I spend my time...
it's where I often get away,
where peace is most sublime.

I place my weary noggin,
upon your billowed chest,
and listen to your heartbeat—
it puts my fears to rest.

It calms my mind and spirit
when're I think of you,
I can only hope that I
have that effect on you.

Remembering

I'm not replacing you,
because that would be an
Impossible thing.
You are, after all,
as you would term it—
inimitable.

You are my favorite
memory,
laughter,
drip of wine,
cookie crumb,
untied shoelace.

I come undone
at the mere thought
of your smile,
your glance,
your touch.

A thousand miles
doesn't matter,
because you are
always right inside
my heart.

UNREQUITED

So I'm going out
with new friends
to a place I think
you'd probably like.

I might order a Malbec
in your honor.

Replacing you?

Never.

Remembering?

Always.

I dreamt my heart was empty,
just an open chamber with empty halls.
You left without saying goodbye, and
nothing but echoes remained.

There was nothing I could do to fill it
back up. Nothing fit or belonged.
So I sat there within those naked walls—
and mourned.

UNREQUITED

Despondent

My inner voice calls to you,
a constant monologue...
telling you the secrets of my heart.

These loving arms open wide,
can't wait for your embrace,
I long for you each day we are apart.

Realization swarms my brain,
my heart and soul as well...
feeling despondent.

Smirk

smɜːk

hɪz ˈbjutəfəl smaɪl
aɪm traɪjɪŋ tu fəˈgɛt...

bʌt aɪm ˈmɛzməraɪzd
ænd ɪnˈtriːgd baɪ
ðæt slaɪ ˈsɪmpə.

ˈlɪtl dɪd aɪ nəʊ
hiː wɒz dʒʌst ˈbiːɪŋ
ænˌtægəˈnɪstɪk.

Smirk

His beautiful smile
I'm trying to forget...

but I'm mesmerized
and intrigued by
that slight simper.

little did I know
he was just being
antagonistic.

Here to Mourn

Did you ever love me at all
or was I just a game to you?
Was I just someone you could use
to boost your massive ego—
then drop the moment I needed you?

Since when was I not allowed to speak?
When did you become so tired
of hearing my voice in your head?
Because I would've gone
through Hell and back for you.

Now, I've been told to be quiet.
That I am too emotional
that I'm too much.
After three years of banter
nearly every day.

I didn't do it to annoy or keep tabs,
I did it because
if I couldn't be next to you,
chatting was the next best thing.
I just wanted to be closer.

Now, there's just an echo
where only my voice remains.

This place that used to be full of love
is empty now.

Now, I just come here to mourn.

BRANDY LANE

Takotsubo Syndrome

I've read of people
dying from a broken heart,
and know that
is probably the one thing
that will finally do me in—
because the pain
of not hearing from you
for even just one day,
is almost unbearable.

I've cried so much
that my vision is blurry,
my chest hurts,
and my heart keeps tripping—
but not like when it used to
skip a beat when you'd
make me happy or look my way,
no... this feels like I'm collapsing,
falling to the earth,
in horrendous pain.

I ate, but I regret it,
because the pit
in my stomach
now feels like
it contains a boulder.

UNREQUITED

My entire body
feels like
it's being squished
and squeezed—
as If a giant
is holding my heart
in its hands
and wringing it out
over and over again.

Tears flood my face
and wet my shirt.
It's as if my body
is trying to purge
every memory of you.

How do I make it stop?
When will it end?

Does all of the joy
that I felt
during the time
that we were together,
come out as pain
now that you
no longer need me
in your life?

Because if so—

I will never feel joy again.

No Longer in Denial

I think I'll give up wine
'cause it makes me think of you—
it makes me sad and teary,
nostalgic, and quite blue.

I quit writing poems,
for the most part, anyway—
although I still fawn over you
every single day.

I quit the chocolate cookies,
you know, with chocolate chips—
'cause it makes me think of how
you lick crumbs off your lips.

I forsook playing games,
because they're no longer fun—
not much teasing anymore,
or taunting that you won.

I no longer get to laugh,
and very rarely smile.
As far as loving you?
I'm no longer in denial.

UNREQUITED

I constantly feel like
I'm banging my head on a wall saying;
"stupid, stupid, stupid... why am I so stupid?"

Can anyone tell me where I messed up so horribly
that I got to where I am?

Is it because I'm too soft? Scared?
That's it... I'm a chicken. I am a flipping chicken.

I let everyone else be happy,
everyone else gets their way
because I'm a softie.
I have a sense of unwavering responsibility...
there is no love in that.

Oh, I had love right in front of me...
I waved at it, blew it kisses, flirted,
and wrote it books of poetry.

But I didn't jump.

My feet were glued to the ground the entire time,
cemented in responsibility.

Oh, how I wish I could've jumped.

Just a Breath

Three years are just a breath,
a gasp...
the little bit of oxygen
in my otherwise
uninhabitable
atmosphere.

You brought me to life,
a spark...
that touched my soul

UNREQUITED

Compass

My compass always points to home,
the destination never changes—
no matter where or far I roam,
though life often rearranges—
my endpoint is always you—
no matter what I say or do.

I've tried to push you from my mind
moved to leave it all behind—
but in my head, you're always there
and I won't act like I don't care.

Your Favorite Book

Hold me like your favorite book;
stare at me for hours and
hang on my every word.

Be excited for each new chapter,
and sad when there's not much
time to sit down with me.

Desire to dive into my pages
over and over again,
like you can never get enough,
and pray that the story
never ends.

UNREQUITED

Turn

Did you really care?

Or was I just
a game you played?

Who won?

Because I don't feel
like the victor.

I have no prize
or trophy,
and you don't seem
to be playing anymore.

As a matter of fact,
I wasn't even aware
that it was my turn.

Unloved

I try my best,
do things for others—
am taken for granted,
overlooked.

I go out of my way
I really should stop
because no one cares-
nonchalant.

Want to be cherished
loved and adored
I thought you did-
but you stopped.

Now I'm nothing.
Absolutely nothing.
Nothing
(except for one thing).

Unloved.

UNREQUITED

Gravity

I miss having my head in the clouds—
all this gravity makes my head hurt.

Used to be I'd have you
to comfort me on occasion.

I miss that.
I miss you.

BRANDY LANE

Concupiscence

At first glance
Cupid's aim
struck my heart;
so I thought...

It drove deep,
through the core
of my soul;
I was bared.

All could see
in my eyes
my desire
to be loved.

Innocent
like a child;
how could that
be a sin?

Love so pure
soul to soul
yet some say
"forbidden".

UNREQUITED

Confession

There's a confession harbored deep within my sub-conscience— whispering to me over and over again;

"You love him."

"I know!" I reply,

but...

*It is tearing me apart inside—
my love for you just won't subside.
My whispered love upon your chest
still lingers on my lips to rest.*

UNREQUITED

Haunt

You haunt me,
and I'm not sure how
because you're still alive...
but I swear—
I can feel your ghost all over me.
I tingle when I think of you.

I feel you go through me,
inside of me,
you are mingling
with my soul.

BRANDY LANE

My Heart Breaks

You're right.
I'm wrong.
I'm so not strong.

The tears...
won't stop!
Drip, drip...drip, drop.

My heart
It aches,
slowly, it breaks.

UNREQUITED

Enough

One day, one moment,
was enough to spark my creativity and self-worth
enabling me to share my words with you.

I will continue to bleed ink onto the pages of books—
telling the world how desperately I love you for as long as I
have breath in my lungs.
Although whispering it with exasperation whilst nuzzling
into your chest is much more exhilarating.

*I think I left my soul on your floor
upon leaving you the other night.*

I'm trying to figure out what I'm supposed to do
because somewhere in the timeline of the many
centuries that I felt I've known you, I must've lost you.
It is all I can do to come to terms with this longing
that I have to care for you, to keep you close—
although trying to keep you wild and free.

It is as if you are a time traveler,
and in those rare moments that we are together,
you and I are the only people in existence.
You are UNFORGETTABLE.

This abundant ache is worth every memory because
they get lots of screentime in my mind.
I could replay your smile over and over again—
or the way you looked at me in church that one Sunday
when we were having cookies.
I remember I was wearing my blue dress
and you looked at me with such adoration.

*No one has ever looked at me the
way you do.*

Truly Wanted

Can I ask you to tell me
all the sweet little lies that you once told me,
for old times' sake?

The ones in which you tell me that I'm pretty
and that you love me?

Can you stare at me as though
you've seen the heavens in my eyes
like you did once, not so long ago?

Because it felt like I was right there with you—
in the presence of God and all of His angels—
whenever you'd look into them.

Just one more time,
to feel your soul entwined with mine?

A mingle? A dance?
Just hold me in your arms and tell me
you don't want me to go.

Please, ask me to stay—
even though you know I will have
to turn you down...

Because along with that soul-crushing ache,
I'll know that I'm truly wanted.

UNREQUITED

Wild Abandonment

What do I have to do
to hear the words I crave—
fall from your lips?

You thought
I couldn't hear you,
but my darling,
I was simply unable to run to you
like I wanted to.

I should've just flown to you
in wild abandonment
when I had the chance!

For now, I am lost,
my mind is crippled,
and I am broken-hearted.

The only thing I long for is your love.

Mind to Mind

Some mornings, I am transported back
to the cold winter mornings
when I made cups of tea and craggy toast—
the days when I would watch the yellow sun
glint off of the freshly fallen snow.

The times in which I would practice music,
and would always find myself in your company—
writing to you as though you were right next to me.

The seasons have come and gone,
come and gone,
and come again.

And here I am,
once again finding myself in your company—
in time and in words on a screen.

We've spent hours together
playing games and feasting,
not to mention the occasional touch,
yet right here is where we've spent the most time—
mind to mind.

Unbreakable

I missed it, didn't I?

That small window of opportunity that you opened—
it's closed now, isn't it?

*I realized too late,
that I am indeed,
in love with you.*

Now, it doesn't matter,
and no matter how hard I try—
the glass is unbreakable.

I Always Will

You called me pretty...
while gazing at me
over a mess of game pieces.

I still float on every compliment,
although it was a while ago.

I remember in your office,
the first time I told you that
I love you.

Those feelings haven't changed.
I still do. I always will.

UNREQUITED

Him.

He makes me want to dance again—
causes my soul to leap every time he's near.

The funny thing is that it is not his physical presence,
but instead, his essence that dances with mine—
that mingles, then slowly tangoes and collides within.

*My heart beats for him here,
in the middle of this life.*

Fading

You're fading from view...
almost like you want to.
Your name was always at the top.
Now, it's not.
I see your little bubble pop up
on the screen,
you've read my message,
it's not unseen...

But—you don't reply.

You see,
usually, I wouldn't care
that there was no response,
because usually,
I would have something on the calendar
to look forward to...
something to do with you,
but there are months of nothing scheduled.
The only thing I have to do
is the same thing I've been doing
for months now...
and that's missing you.

You can't change that...

UNREQUITED

I still miss my first dog
and my favorite cat!

I still miss my very first love.

I will miss you until the day I die.
because that is how I'm wired.

So go on, ignore me...
but know this,
when you decide not to—

I'll still be here, loving you.

Balconies

I stare out the window
across the way
to empty balconies,
and I wonder if I
will ever be invited
to sit on one.
To have coffee
or a glass of wine
and game nights.

I wonder if I'll be
able to cope
knowing I left
my world behind.
I don't even know
if it would welcome me back.
This one hasn't...
old friends have moved on,
I'm just "somebody that
they used to know."

UNREQUITED

I cringe at the thought
that those I hold dear
will think the same of me.
How can't I keep
the fires burning
from such a distance?
My soul aches
for its companion,
a thousand miles away.

I want to believe
that our friendship
is iron-clad.
I may be out of reach
of your arms
but my soul is yours
always.

Hibernation

Maybe all is not lost here,
such love as this never dies,
but instead, goes tucked away for
when it's needed the most.
Alive in hibernation,
waiting to be awakened.

Vanquish

How empty is a world where I cannot fly—
where paints are limited, and the views are obfuscated.
I miss the sun in all of its glory,
my face looking toward it, beaming.

My heart, a lonely echo in the fading winter,
knowing that spring will not bring respite—
but more echoes.
Tears fall to no avail, and there is nothing I can do to hold
the clock hands in place.

Time marches on like a funeral dirge,
my hope has gone, and I cannot seem to recover it.
Hope, return to me—you cannot leave me this way!

I paint a false smile to wear as a mask.

No more do my eyes bear a secret joy,
as the Mona Lisa—a joy that could not be contained.

Alas—sometimes precious things are broken
and cannot be repaired or replaced,
nor should they be—as that is what made them
so precious to begin with!

To wish for a time machine would be in vain,
I look forward to my dreams to vanquish this pain.

Halfway Blooming

Frozen in time
melancholy frost
from early autumn nights
that chill the air.

Nipping harshly
at my outer petals.
I cannot last
without your warmth.

I will not survive
without your
happy smile
beaming down on me.

Your time is
less and less each day,
the time
you spend with me.

The cold
and lonely nights
are leaving me stranded,
stuck in time.

What will become of me
without your love,
without you to chide me
into opening up?

UNREQUITED

I was so timid before,
but you comforted me into growing,
and I have grown so much inside.

Maybe my timing wasn't quite right,
because inside, I am bursting
with so much that I want to give...

My fragrance, my beauty,
my petals swaying on the breeze
trying to catch your attention.

Alas, I'm afraid you've gone too quickly!

I'm afraid I will only wilt away
on this cold and lonely night without you here.

I nod my head in silence,
I cannot take it anymore!
I succumb to the sad realization
that you have left me...

halfway blooming.

Without

All I want to do is write to you,
unhindered like before...
I don't want to stay dammed up,
this awful ache within my chest.

I want to fly, to have no fear,
I want to dive
into the depths of the ocean
and greet you every day.

Why must I apologize
for this unimaginable joy
I have when I think of you?

My only pain
is when I'm without,
when I am starved
and told I am not allowed...
that gnawing, wretchedness
that my doting words turn into
when they cannot be set free?

Eating me from my insides
and ravishing my brain
like, wayward zombies?

Do I need a hypnotist?

I don't want one!

UNREQUITED

I love the way I feel
when I write with this passion,
this zeal, this zest.

If I have to do it in secret
for the rest of my life,
so be it!
I'll lose everything to have this ability...
this superpower, if you will.

Promise

Every time I try to write to you,
there is a door that slams shut.
I feel as though I am lacking honesty in my feelings—
because I can no longer say what I am feeling.

What are these restrictions upon me?

Why is my soul in chains?

Earthly bounds were one thing,
and a tethered heart, another...
now, the windows of my mind
have been closed
and I'm forever staring out.

What evil have I done but to love?
Isn't that God's greatest commandment?
Why can I no longer write about these emotions?

How are they so wrong if they make up all that I am?

If feeling this way means
that I am no longer allowed to love freely—
and express that outwardly,
then what is the point of living at all?

UNREQUITED

This throbbing pain within my chest,
the angst within my very spirit,
the arguments within my brain...
keeping me from enjoying anything at all.

Love lies forever
entombed in my heart,
eternally bouncing
off of its stone enclosure.

How long until I succumb
to the bleakness?
How long until love
will crack through again
and light up my world?

Why would you throw away
the keys to my heart like that?
Is it that you cannot handle its brightness?

You could no more block out the sun...
the clouds may come,
but not for long,
and my heart refuses to turn to stone.

Love will prevail,
come hell or high water,
I promise.

I Close My Eyes

I awoke in pain, alone...
but not longing for
the absent occupant of
the space beside me.

Pleasure being subservient to pain,
my hands embraced my very flesh,
I closed my eyes and thought of you,
the keeper of my heart and soul.

Waves of warmth to hide the pain...
I was lost for a time in the thought
of your large yet slender fingers,
brushing my hair from my cheek.

That flirty smirk,
the one that crosses your face
when e'er you look upon me.
In my mind, I am lost in you.

Oh, you try so hard to push me away...
but you don't really want to.
You think of me all of the time,
as I do of you.

UNREQUITED

Why can't we ever be?
Just steal away to somewhere
that no one would ever know?
Uncontainable joy for an afternoon?

Because...
It would change everything,
ruin everything,
destroy everything.

So the reality is that you...
will never be mine.
So my hands
once again embrace my flesh,
and I close my eyes.

Temptation

That one summer—
every time our eyes
would fall upon each other's...
I would transport to a time
in which all I knew
was him.

He was my essence,
my garden of life;
full of everything I needed,
including temptation.

But I'm a good girl...
I stayed away
from the succulent sweetness
of those lips,
although I stayed close enough
to become intoxicated
on the fragrance.

I starved myself of everything else,
the "what if" was divine.

Alas,
one cannot live with no sustenance,
and the drunken fragrance succumbed to rot.
I was left hungover and craving
what I could never have...

Him.

UNREQUITED

If My Soul Could Speak

If my soul could speak, uninhibited,
and without being filtered
by my heart or mind...
it would have flown to yours
the moment we met.

It never would've left
your presence,
mingling eternally
with yours.

Instead, my heart is torn,
my mind distorted with thoughts
and reality,
and too many restraints
stand in my way.

It now feels trapped,
screaming at me daily,
fighting to get out
to be with you.

What I first thought
would be heaven,
has turned to a hell
I cannot escape...
maybe upon meeting you...
I sold my soul to the devil.

Forbidden

Oh! I just can't hold it in anymore...
I am just overflowing with love for you.
I feel like I'm going to burst into a billion pieces if I don't write it down. I know it's unrequited, I know it's forbidden, I know it is all on my own that this feeling exists only in my mind... but I do not care! I love the way I feel when I write with you on my mind.
It's better than the angst I carry when I am silent.

Syncopation

The sugar isn't sweet,
nor the salt savory...
the air is rather stale,
champagne's not bubbly.
The wine tastes a bit tart,
a bit like vinegar...
And as for the chocolate?
I'm fatter than before.

The skip in my step left.
My smile disappeared.
Since the day you vanished,
the days have felt like years.
Sleep is hard to come by
I ache for it all day...
for a chance to see you
while I sleep the nights away.

Oh! How I long to hold you
just one more time!
Without you in my life
It holds no reason or no rhyme!
My heart has lost its rhythm
new syncopation than before...
Nothing brings me joy now,
I'll just be sad forevermore.

I Miss You

I miss you in the night,
in the light,
deep in passion's height.

I miss you all the time,
in sips of wine,
when I'm feeling rather fine.

I miss you when I'm not supposed to...
although I've tried to forget,
it seems my mind won't let you go,
my heart's not ready yet.

I miss you when I'm happy,
I miss you when I'm sad...
so much that when I think of you,
it makes my sadness glad.

I guess have to keep this feeling
locked deep down inside,
because I'm not ready to forget you,
my love has not yet died.

When you're not by my side,
I more than miss you...
and it took me awhile to figure out
this feeling.

I finally realized what it really is:
when we're apart...
I'm homesick for you.

Without You

Without you in my life,

I'm like a solar-powered light
without the sun...

A burger
without the bun...

Louisiana
without the Cajun...

Attila
without the Hun...

Blue wine
without the nun..

A joke
without the pun...

A sitcom
without the rerun...

Life's just not much fun.

UNREQUITED

Time With You

If I could make a wish right now,
in hopes that it'd come true.
It would be that I could have
some time to spend with you.

I don't need any more in this life,
no treats, or flowers, or presents
the only thing I tangibly need
is your wonderful presence.

I have searched high, and very low
and into every depth,
when you're not around, I tend to frown,
it truly is akin to death.

So for every wish, from now 'til the end
I will repeat 'til the end of time,
I just want you, and only you...
and I'll wish it until you're mine.

Echo

There's not one thing
I expect from you...
just hear my lament,
hear my cry
so that I know
I'm not alone!

Echo back to me
in the chaos of this world
that you are there!
Even though I know
that this cry
bounces off of you,
I will know
I'm no longer alone...
for the spirits around me
are grumbling.

I long to escape
this wretched existence!
I need the warmth
and love of your soul
to comfort me!

UNREQUITED

I miss the crown
you gently place on my head
to wear in your presence!

The feeling
of humility I have
while you douse me
in respect
and beautiful compliments!

Most of all,
I miss how light
my steps become,
how weariness fades.

Your energy
always fulfills me
and lifts me.

Being There

You are the magic
that unleashes my mind,
tethers my heart,
nourishes my soul.

You vanquish the demons
and light the fire
that shows me the way.

You are the catapult
to my many ideas
and dreams
and desires,
and I am able
to try new things
with my newfound courage.

You don't even need
to hold my hand,
just you being here
is all I need.

No one has ever just
"been there."

Not without judging me, anyway.

You gaze upon me
as though I am art—
speechless.

Then, leave me hanging,
with no audible praise.

Just Like You

Cool air wafts over my bare legs,
its chilly fingers caressing my bare skin.
I long for comfort, for home, for you.

There's something different
about mornings here.
Who am I kidding?
Nothing is the same.
I've tried to reconstruct what I can,
but there is no replicating what I once had;

The trickle of the little creek outside my
window that reflected the sun to greet me—
like little fairies that would flit across my ceiling.

Your voice on Sunday mornings,
singing in the choir.
I listened every Sunday,
if for nothing else than to hear you sing.

The feel of my bed quilt,
that is seemingly irreplaceable.
The one that felt like velvety dragon wings
that would hold me through the night.

My comfy Papasan,
the one you cozied up in
on a few occasions for movies...
I loved that chair,
but even more so when you were in it.

UNREQUITED

Things change,
I suppose it is inevitable.

I also suppose that others have felt as I do,
wanting to somehow solidify a moment,
to keep it the same; paintings, pictures,
movies, poetry...
all vain attempts to keep a moment, a
memory, an era, a lesson.

Like drawings in a cave,
we try so hard to keep stories alive,
to remember the feelings that we had
in those moments.

We try to convey those feelings to others,
not just because
they are nearly impossible to contain,
but because we want others
to share in our joy,
and our pain.
I suppose that is what makes us
uniquely human

I simply try to start over.
When all seems lost,
I remember that there's this paintbrush...
and I begin to paint again.

CONTINUED
...

BRANDY LANE

New can be just as beautiful,
yet, uniquely different.

What beautiful moments I had before
can never be replicated,
nor would I want them to be.
They were rare, precious, and wonderful.

To try to copy them
would make them "less than."

Today, I am through mourning what I had.
I will always cherish the memories,
and will look forward to making many new ones.
I know that I'm not through telling stories,
and you will forever be a character,
even if not directly;
because you are forever a part of me now.

Everything I do has a touch of you in it.
You added colors to my palette
that cannot be duplicated—
and those colors can now be seen
in everything I paint.

I suppose it is a vibrant,
almost neon shade of blue.
Calming, yet exciting.
Quiet, yet charismatic.
A walking contradiction.

Just like you.

Wild Things

I'm just a dumb girl.
One that got caught up in your sweetness.
One that craved you a little too much.

Sometimes, I forget that you will never be mine
and I try to hold you a little too tightly.

I forgot you cannot keep wild things.
Wild things need to be free.

I didn't even realize I was grasping so tightly,
until I noticed some of the iridescence
rubbing off onto my fingers—
just like when I held butterflies
as a child.

Forgive me for holding on too tight,
I suppose I'd gotten so used to everyone leaving me,
that I forgot to trust that you wouldn't as well.

Teardrops

How much time within
a teardrop does flow?
Can someone measure?
Does anyone know?

If time were counted
in buckets and mugs,
or wrung-out tee shirts
from long, tear-stained hugs,

would we count the years
that were the best too?
The ones that I got
to spend time with you?

If I'd have to grieve
the joy that I've found,
there'd be one large sea,
not any dry ground.

We all would be lost
in that briny sea...
because tears would flow
for eternity.

The Train

The lonely whistle of the train
cries longingly of home...
It travels fast and far and wide,
and through the cities roams.

Each time I hear it's brazen sound,
I feel a bit unraveled.
To think of all the many miles
that the train has traveled.

Pondering the sights and sounds,
the traffic that it's stopped,
the many loads of packages,
and passengers it's dropped.

I think of how easily
I could hop a train,
and pray that it goes by your house,
so I could see you again.

I'd sit with cows or cars or coal,
uncomfortable for miles...
If it would mean my destination
was in the presence of your smile.

Irreplaceable

I'm dying inside!
I don't know how I'm going to do this
without you near.

I adore you in ways
that I've never experienced
with anyone else...

and no experience
will ever be the same.

You are irreplaceable.

UNREQUITED

Pieces of Me

You take a little here, a little there...
My poetry, my recipes, my joy.

You use my energy, my peace,
My love, my time...

I gave them freely,
only to be left with nothing...
because you acted without
reciprocating...

Just like everyone else.

Dragon Tears

Can I borrow you for a moment?
You see, my dragon has flown away
and I cannot seem to focus
on anything beautiful lately...
mainly because the beautiful
is hard to see through all of my tears.

I'm rather forlorn, and my lifeblood overflows
with emotion and the blackest of ink
with which to write it all down,
but without my dragon to comfort me,
and the quietness of our little cave,
all of my writing has turned dull and gray.

My colors are all gone,
and nothing but cold ashes are left
where the fires were burning.

I thought, maybe,
you could pretend to be him...
maybe you could sit with me in my mind
and nap whilst I work?

He never said much anyway,
a new word here or there
and grumbles about eating, mostly.

UNREQUITED

I don't know why it became
so cozy there
but I've had trouble
with expressing my words
ever since the day he left.

He was somehow— magical, brilliant,
beautiful and ornery—all at once.

Most days, I don't know
what to say anymore—as I feel like
I've abandoned him somehow.
But I am only trying to be respectful.

I glance up at the cave
and imagine the light turned on—
him cozy and working
and waiting for me
to bring a happy note or dessert.

He's just no longer there
and I miss him dreadfully.

Awaiting a Frolic

It has been quite some time since I heard your voice, yet this morning—the reminiscent sweetness of your words echoed inside of my skull.

Washing my face, brushing the mop of hair atop my head, not quite ready for the day—I looked into the mirror and heard your voice telling me;

"You're so pretty!"

I haven't been privy to those words in quite a while...

I needed to hear that today—your sweet words picked me up like a Phoenix out of the ashes.

I glossed my lips, lengthened my lashes, slicked my hair into a ponytail, and put on a pretty dress. The gown is navy chiffon with bright red, orange, and yellow flowers amongst vibrant green leaves—much like a field of summer blossoms awaiting a frolic. Then realized that no matter how much I wish for it, you won't just magically appear, and that it is much too cold for my new pretty dress.

So, I am writing to you instead, whilst all dressed up, to spend a few moments writing to you before I don something a little warmer and a little less gossamer.

Someday, I will be sure to wear it when I finally have your company, but for now, it is going back on the hanger—to wait for that day.

Hopefully, it won't be too long.

UNREQUITED

I want to wear
a pretty dress,
one that reminds me of
the days of old.

I want to wander in
the forests,
and keep company
with dragons.

I did—
once upon a time,
and I still believe
in happy endings...

Brandy Lane

About the Author

Brandy Lane

Brandy Lane has lived most of her life in Indiana and Colorado, where she has raised four beautiful children. She published her first book, *Where Beautiful Loves*, in December 2020 under her imprint, Where Beautiful Inks. Just after the release of her first book, she discovered anthologies as an option for publishing and has since had poetry pieces included in over three dozen publications. In 2023, she curated and edited, *Winter, A Poetic Anthology* which is a collaboration of 25 poets from all over the world. It spent 5 days at #1 in New Releases in Anthologies on Amazon. A hopeless romantic, Brandy draws inspiration mainly from nature, but also from human connection.

Her poetry is much like her personality, showing vulnerability as well as strength. The muse that she writes to is someone who taught her she is worthy of love, that she is "enough" and yes, "sometimes more than enough."

She finds beauty in every situation, which sometimes is her greatest curse. In her spare time, she loves spending time outdoors in the mountains, taking in the sublime views. She also loves a good board game, acting, singing, and video chatting with her favorite friends all over the world. Brandy can be found online: on Instagram @wherebeautifullives and Facebook @Where Beautiful Lives

About the Editor

Valerie Lorraine

Valerie Lorraine is an author of poetry. She has 2 published books of her poetry collections, and 2 previous anthologies that includes a heathy body of work from a total of 24 beautiful Poets. She continues to work on more books which include both her own work & more anthologies. Valerie works as an Editor, Writing Coach and Self-Publishing Consultant. Her goal is to direct & encourage those who desire to create a legacy with their pen & their heart. She helps them bring the vision of their art to life. As an advocate, Valerie gently offers her message. She encourages strength & self love for survivors of domestic violence & emotional trauma. It is a message she wishes she didn't understand, but is well aware it helped create the person she is proud of today. Valerie is extremely active as a host & mentor. To find out more, Valerie Lorraine can be found on Instagram @valerielorraineproductions Books by Valerie can be found on Amazon at amazon.com/author/valerie_lorraine

Forward Written by:
Stevie Flood

Residing on the beautiful Maltese Islands, Stevie Flood has captivated most of her magnificent essence in writing, by the attention of no other than the landscapes alone. Seasonal changes on the island bring out her colourful pieces of ink to light.

At the ripe old age of four, Stevie began her literacy journey. Very special thanks to her father, Peter Flood, who always encouraged her on a whole other level – to be inspired by the outside world around her, and detail it to its very core of how magnificent ink could be, if it is described down to the very last drop of ink, in her mind only then the story will be complete.

Making her life as full as can be, these fine pieces of ink were motivated by unfortunate events, and now slowly shimmering memories remain of the man she writes her pieces to. If you would love to find out more and read more of her amazing poetry, just look her up on:

Facebook at: https://www.facebook.com/stevie.floodauthor/
Instagram: https://www.instagram.com/stevie.flood/
TikTok: https://www.tiktok.com/@stevieflood4

Acknowledgments

So grateful for the editors and publishers that have included the following poems in their anthologies and magazines. The poems, many times in their rawest and earliest versions, appeared as follows.

Teardrops (pg. 174) **was first seen in** *The Briny Sea of Poetry* **also written by the author.**

Also Published In

Poetry 365 by RDW (both abridged and unabridged editions) for November, December, January, February, March, April, May, and June, and special editions of *Creator*, *Hope*, and *Self Portrait* editions.

Red Penguin Books has published her pieces in *'Tis the Season's*, *The Flower Shop on the Corner*, *The Ocean Waves*, and *Bloom* Issue 2 magazine.

Clarendon House Publications published her poems in their *Poetica 2* and *Poetica 3* anthologies.

Ink Gladiators Press' anthologies of *The Rise and Fall of Chimera's* and *Gray, We Hide our Colors Within*.

Indie Blu(e) Publishing published a mental health piece in *Through the Looking Glass: Reflecting on Madness and Chaos Within*, and their newest anthology, *But You Don't Look Sick: The Real Life Adventures of Fibro Bitches, Lupus Warriors, and Other Superheroes Battling Invisible Illness*.

300 South Media Group has published her in *As Darkness Falls* and features her first flash fiction piece in *Sunset Rain*. She will also have three pieces included in *Shadow of the Soul*.

Train River Poetry has published her in *Poetry 7*.

Who's Who of Emerging Writers by **Sweetycat Press.**

Harness Magazine in their November 2022 issue.

Silent Spark Press *Amazing Poetry* Volume 13, 2023.

Other books by Brandy Lane:

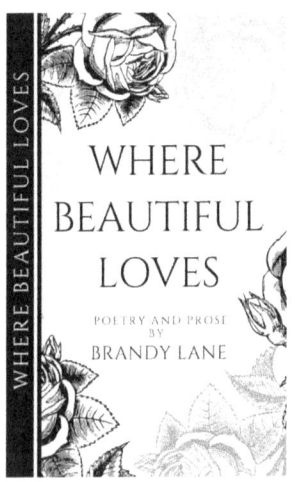

In the Works

www.ingramcontent.com/pod-product-compliance
Lightning Source LLC
Chambersburg PA
CBHW052139070526
44585CB00017B/1895